dead boy

Jason Morphew

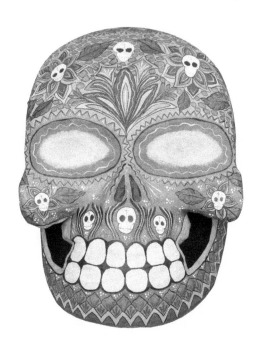

Spuyten Duyvil

New York City

©2018 Jason Morphew
ISBN 978-1-944682-90-3
Cover design: Carrick Moore Gerety
Back cover painting Black Face Daddy: Matilda Saffron Morphew

Library of Congress Cataloging-in-Publication Data

Names: Morphew, Jason, author.
Title: Dead boy / Jason Morphew.
Description: New York City : Spuyten Duyvil, [2018]
Identifiers: LCCN 2017038932 | ISBN 9781944682903 (softcover)
Classification: LCC PS3613.O755255 A6 2018 | DDC 811/.6--dc23
LC record available at https://lccn.loc.gov/2017038932

Dedication

For enemies
dead before
my birth—
I wrote this
in your worried arms
of magic.

RIGHT EYE

Left Eye

Right Eye

How to Write a Poet's Bio

Love a genre
lyric a throne of leaves
narrative a noose
a bio's not a poem.
Write that down. Most things aren't.
Were you born
someplace? Slip that in.
Will you die someplace else?
Up to you. Dress to impress
the robot made of roses
humming like a humanist.
Are your poems high
enough to hangover?
You'll want to stab
discerning eyes with a dirty edge of that.
Are your poems clean as heaven?
Dark as birth canal?
Then don't forget
you're not your poems
you're so far away
and it's a reader's job
to see.

House of David

I could not go where you were going
and your vanishing
so inarticulate
generates religions
whose only holy man
and mystic
singing on another plane
is me.

Innocence/Perversity

The right way is the wrong way

my daughter age 1

dead boy

you wouldn't know it

        to look at him

racquet swinging kitchen dancing baby

        lifting not alive

pulse faked by metronome

        love faked by time

every smile a figment

        of an anonymous

        mind

At the Disneyland Hotel

I found myself
alone
in the lobby
with Goofy—
two costumes
juxtaposed:
Fame and Obscurity
Animal and Man.
We stood in our
manufactured faces
wordlessly acknowledging
the security
at the exits.

marriage

babies cry in the womb—

practicing

doctors say.

I think of you and me

(voluntary twins)

passing in the hall

children weeping

in our arms—

aren't they still practicing?

are we?

Baby in a Blender

The day after she miscarried
again we stumbled into Macy's
our matrimonial blender
was dead   we identified
then clutched the most
expensive one they had
a Vitamix   brought it home
and blended everything in sight
beets rhubarbs raspberries wine
music mortgage manuscript
our nanny watching with a frightened look
as if remembering the playground
jokes about the quality of red
spinning
everything mixed with everything else
all those vitamins
nourishing the earth
pulling it out   putting it inside
love is hilarious
and immature
my lips covered with blood.

My Youth

I walked with a zombie
who followed commands
on an island
of revolutionary slaves
who were always writing
true songs
and apologizing for them.
Every saint was black and gay
full of arrows.
Births were mourned
deaths celebrated.
One god at a time came down.
Rich whites suffered
while fingering keyboards.
Nothing good or beautiful
mindlessness spreading
electroshock therapy prescribed.
White boys either stalked
the edge of alcoholism
or begged white girls
not to love them.
The only store with anything
white boys wanted
was called *Nigger Liquor.*
I walked with a transgender zombie.
Long flowing auburn hair
caressed its neatly groomed beard.
I don't know if the zombie ever found a way
to stuff itself inside the trembling
neglected women who squeezed so tightly
their eyes closed when they pleaded
for it to enter in.
What I know is I walked with it

I knocked on nearby doors
and asked the poor if they knew it.
I wore pleated slacks and penny loafers
to walk with it and ask.
What impressed the islanders
about the zombie was it kept living
after being killed. That's what a zombie is.
It lives on but it's different. It doesn't speak.
It watches. It's got a god inside.
The bloated islanders dying young
thought following the zombie
would make them zombies too.
They were in the zombie's entourage
hoping it was contagious.
The island was full of huge hospitals
named for black gay saints
no one knew were black or gay.
The saints made sure every patient died.
When I was twenty and left the island
the ferry captain told me
Better doctors are required.

Evangelical Christianity

No horror is horror
until it is

escaped

carried with you
into your child's face

cross spinning in the DNA
cross rising in the pool
murder moving

through the heart of love.

Acute and Chronic

after *Fallen* by Lauren Kate

My daughter explodes
when told it's time for dinner
her childhood interrupted
by mundane survival.
Did kids explode
before childhood was invented
when no one expected
to do anything but survive
and there was no need
to relinquish plastic duck
molded into medical doctor
holding tiny reflex hammer
wearing white coat and head mirror?
Maybe that quack was about to save her life
who am I to disrupt any diagnosis
it's out of my testicles
now her ferocious life
all I do is usher her into and out of
a little cloud of smoke
trying not to rupture its delicate ringlets
knowing one day I'll return to it
alone.

Leslie

I loved a girl called Leslie
who hated having her name
pronounced *Lezlee.*
"It's an S" she'd say and turn
and curve away.
Now when someone says *lezbo*
I am offended
for Leslie and for softness
and I regret the many ways
I have insulted love.

After I Write My Dissertation

I shall compose
a series of mystery novels
featuring the Traveling Wilburys.
Each Wilbury will embody
a paranormal expertise—
Roy Orbison is a zombie
with the power
to freeze murderers
with his crystal voice.
Tom Petty can chew
through any substance
with his diamond teeth.
Jeff Lynne baffles
disappears behind
his Beard of Invisibility.
George Harrison's accent
separates evildoers' skin
from their bone and tissue.
Dylan has no discernable talent.
He spends the mystery
drinking brandy and ridiculing
what everyone else is doing
saying things like
Great idea and *Smooth move.*
Dylan you prick
the man who grooms
Jeff Lynne's beard
during down time back at the mansion
is known to say.
But on the penultimate page
Dylan always prevents
a Wilbury from walking off a ledge
or into farmers' market traffic

surprising the others
with his capacity
for love.

Then they sum up everything
that's happened
in a song
just north of mediocre
whose existence
is a miracle
like entering a nursing home
and finding someone
you know.

Authenticity

"Bail hearing set for man arrested wearing
fake suicide vest..."
AP Feb 17 2012

How far can one travel
on the edge of indecision
effortlessly circling the sun
a satellite generating dissertation topics
a terroirist dancing the twelvestep
with an oversized Czech—
suicide is style
to poets and to atoms
death is language
in cosmopolitan complacencies
and Rockefeller Privies
a fist of caviar
in a formaldehidden face.
Hard things have happened
it's soft to be alive.

Physical Comedy

Your death is funny
a wrong turn
onto a road that isn't there.
You misjudge the distance
between your body
and hereafter
and it's funny the little slip
that splits you
the little slip that stops you
the little slip
from everything there is.
Dick Van Dyke the Grim Reaper
John Ritter the Grim Reaper
Jesus Christ the Grim Reaper
of the Grim Reaper
every decomposing bone
making snapping sounds at once
every human face passing
through windshields
into every elm tree in the world.
This is a comedy
because the ending
is happening.

Mascots

for Fritz

Common to say
all players go through
slumps in their careers—
but what if
the greatest hitter there ever was
entered a slump at birth
and never pulled out?
What could be said of him?
What could he possibly feel?
Why would any team
allow him to live on
much less clothe feed
and encourage him
yet again to try?
Such generosity
is evil on this cruel island
generating shame
so paralyzing
the greatest hitter there ever was
lies motionless
as another face grows
slowly over his own—
permanent smile dead eyes
strange spots and lines
decorating a second skin—
platypus among the homonyms
boos and *booze*
swinging singing
winners hate to lose.

How I Came to Stay in The Hague of My Heart

In the fancy hick halfjungle of my youth

I spraypainted my name on box turtles

so when I tripped on them again

en route to shoot doves with air

rifles dip Skoal jerk off to bodies buried

in exhumed magazines

my creeping signature might

interrupt empire

causing a pausing to reflect on feelings

and mercy hence the irony

of these iron chains preventing

all my love.

No blues

describes only love
always it's revealed

the singer's broke
on a broken train
in a brackish world
with an impure mind

I need your
love is free
and I'm broke

freedom means oⁿ

money required
them aristocratic atom blues
as smashed in

Poverty + Leisure
amuse me
unless you have some

torture
I'll pay you back

Does James Brown have a penis?

she asks from her pink toilet
holding in one hand a plastic idol
of the singer and in the other its
corresponding microphone.
Well   hard to describe genitalia of the dead
men have penises. She gazes at Godfather
of Soul toward the eternal
I take it from her trying to see:
paleblue moundrise paleblue crotch
nothing settled everything obscure
I give the legend back
and mysteriously announce
Men and boys have penises. Increased nuance
same result daughter's eyes daring doll
to swerve as in videos
just ended. As she stands I want to say
The soul's outside the body
the soul's outside the world
after your bath when you're exhausted
and I drape you in a towel
I am an attending flame
but you are the blaze already
roaring past my arms
my hands my name.

Abortifacient

Several sazeracs later
he was not sorry he had been born
he was sorry he was ever born
everywhere all the time.
So he made another sazerac
knowing he could not make it
stop but only partially deformed
he must try to slow it down.

For the mature gentleman at the Studio City CVS

who said *You're not invisible*
thank you
for being insane
I want to be there with you
waiting for prescriptions
connected to a name
by condescending whitecoats
aglow against candy
and Canadian whisky
really there with a chip card
a miracle a man a
biological tease

instead of the universe
obscuring
the drug from the disease.

National Poetry Month

longer than Black History Month
though poetry black and brief
should be blacker briefer—
give poetry a National Nanosecond
hide it at all other times
don't speak of it in schools
or make it on your smartphone
pretend it isn't there
until the yearly pulse arrives—
then uncover then make naked
every poem even half conceived
so the world superfluous
forever disappears.

field song

seed of death within me
floating over hidden notches
seed of death within me
where no doctor watches
seed of death within me
does not require water
seed of death within me
cares not about my daughter
seed of death within me
subjectively a dancer
seed of death within me
objectively a cancer
seed of death within me
fleck of shadowed mountain
seed of death within me
drop from blackened fountain
seed of death within me
my blood is flowing soil

reading in darkness

climbing a falling ladder

drunking a fuck model

praying for silence

adulterating a child

sipping blood from

dead ideas

rusting twilight

sky

Winery

Spring 2009

Yesterday as I trained the young couple
I saw that one could not be without the other
they couldn't bear a moment's separation
knew nothing about wine
had finals the next day at Sac State
where they took the same classes
studying each other.
I told them to tell me if their
shared mind had a question
it's best to learn by doing so
they flirted as Chuck the security guard
did a hammered tasting for confused customers
and I read a novel in the kitchen
glass of our finest cabernet in hand.

I opened another bottle.
Suddenly Chuck was reading his own novel
across the kitchen table from me.
It was my suicidal friend's twentyseventh birthday
the rock star death year.
My fiancée and I had just been to Orlando to hear
her uncle's hundred asynchronous
cuckoo clocks chime adopted daughters
into manhood another friend
had just been to Orlando to identify
the body of his father who died by
leap from airport parking deck.

I got that friend a job at the winery when we all got back from Orlando.
The next day the winery sent an email saying it was closing down.
My fiancée and I are getting married at the winery two weeks after it closes.
The young couple is getting married two weeks from today. That's illegal.
My boss calls Chuck my boyfriend because
I pour him drinks and listen to
his three stories six hundred times an hour.
He has a teenage daughter he has never seen. I am her invisible stepfather.

One half of the young couple dropped a case of our most expensive chardonnay.
Every bottle shattered. The couple looked at me in horror
Chuck bleared up from his novel to see what I would do.
What I did was think darkness is illuminated by storms.

Halogen

Three years ago we came
to the house of twelve million track lights
which live slickly two years
as if powered by hamster
earning master's degree.
Lately climbing the ladder
at six AM to replace another individual
aspect of the whole
as my son slowly pours milk onto the dining table
and my daughter shrieks *I don't like this song!*
groping through the growing abrogation
I wonder if this light will outlive me
this prosthetic of my mind
symbol of my striving
crafted far away by someone else.

Regret

I want to find everyone

I should have had sex with

set them side by side

in my living room

and sadly fuck them

one by one—

then I'll bring in those

I should not have touched

and erase myself

by being numb

among them

all of us forgetting

we ever dreamed

we aren't alone.

Torment

I am riding a Greyhound bus
from Memphis to Nashville
concerned about the integrity
of my coffee cup which slowly leaks
eighteen year old Highland Park
a gift from my wife's publisher
for debuting at number one
on the New York Times Bestseller List.
She rides a jet in first class and is
almost already in Nashville.
It is 9:12 am.
My wife is not yet thirty years old.
I am thirty seven.
It was lucky I was late
I got an emptier bus.
So many travel this route
on Fridays an overflow coach
is required. I exceed
I am too much. Here's my problem:
if I drink the entire bottle
it will shock my wife
and it will be rather selfish
though her publisher only sent this vintage
because he and I drank it together
in Berlin as she sipped Riesling
making everybody
money.
There are other problems.
I have lost a library book
I need for my dissertation.
It contains ingenious marginalia
that might have made me famous
for something other than drinking

ashes of the Bebelplatz.
In Memphis we stayed at the Peabody
The South's Grand Hotel.
Everyone was hammered.
That was the dress code.
Now in carpeted seats behind me
black youths debate virtues
of the Bonaroo Music Festival.
I thought only fools liked jam bands
I thought blacks could not be fools.
I am a snob on a Greyhound
sipping scotch from a disintegrating cup.
I am famous for drinking.
This is a limousine.
The driver carries a chauffeur's license.
The bus is now almost empty
but we will take on other riders
who will frustrate our expectations
as we have frustrated
anyone who has loved us
enough
to be surprised.

Passion

In ten years
I'll think I was a fool
to entertain thoughts
of ever dying
ten years past
that I won't recall
how I feel today
naked
but for compression stockings
whitewhiskered in a Sydney
hotel room eating codeine
drinking screwdrivers
for
which
my wife's publisher shall pay.
She rides white Rolls
in Blue Mountains
discussing inspiration
en
route
to thronged events.
Here I Sheraton
I doublefist the room
approaching no
place I am
the event as young
as I have ever been
handwriting the same.
A bandage obscures my navel
for I was born this morning
from the minibar
a parallel wound
from another hemisphere

even more Southern
already a man
with no appendix
no gesticulation
beyond what goes
unseen today.

Never Settle

said the house to the patent troll
to the feather on the wave
never
leave the bed in hands
of the afternoon
never ever
love to live.
Put what you have on a gelded ghost
shoot it in its broken leg
initialize a claim
on a shallow family plot
in a field of mud
across the racist road
from a dollar store.
Never settle
for what's happening.
The beetle that will know you
isn't yet a twinkle
on the edge of embalmed genitalia
there still sparkles a Jacuzzi
of time to curse
and cross.

Plastic Texas

Where is the awful poem
from the journal that rejected me
about Texas made of plastic bags
swirling in the ocean?
It was so long and so bad
I crossed out everything superfluous
leaving only facts foraged from newspaper.
I'm delving for those details now
diving through my desperation
which is the waist
high rejectoral college stacked by the toilet
in my office.

I don't need facts or poems
to pack my bags for Plastic Texas
to catch my mail from passing planes
sliding each jagged journal
into its own sack and sinking
slowly in my independent palace
I will do the sea a service
obscuring shocking garbage
revealing a new and relevant Atlantis
where invisible poems downward
twist forgetting ever wanting
to be seen.

Avalanche

Somewhere above
cold plans
to bury you
dead boy
ice arcing
like a rainbow
to your eyes
God's promise
never to flood the world
with love to keep
life a terrible surprise.

Alibi

I'm not capable
of hatred
my concentration
flags.
I create families
sleep and dream
of vertical snakes
airborne on a river
searching all of Arkansas
for New Medusa's mind.
My exstepfather floats
in a ridiculing canoe
beside me
offering a loaded gun
on the flat end of an
extended oar.

Snakes will stay
or complete their motion
regardless of my attention.
Redneck gangsters
homeless hit men
roam
unhired.
Billions of legs
go unbroken.
I go unpoisoned
unprisoned
laughing at appropriate times.

Who can know what happens?

Able to imagine nothing

more shallow
than saying *I love you*
to my dying father
yet needing to be shallow
I leaned in and listed
every way he hurt me
as if David whispered
to Michelangelo
how the chisel felt.

Strange

finally to be perceived
as old as one has always felt
winning the argument
slowly in others' eyes.
What now? Am I *really* mortal?
If so why this

Let's take it apart

and see what happens
my twoyearold son says
kneeling naked at a Casio
keyboard speaker plugged
into an iPhone resting
on a rock up the slope
of our Laurel Canyon
backyard. My God is
he an engineer? Please
let him be an engineer
save him from the curse
of creativity of whoring
out the heart and mind
on spec to gormless johns
who neither understand nor
pay. Save him from poetry
and music deliver him from
dreams of hammocked spray
into mahogany and money
made of leather flowers
cascading down the opened robes
of the young and sideways
slick. Get him laid God
not too often despite
his shocking dick.
Dare I think it?
Make him happy
as he is here loving
loved and nude.
Dad you're Bacchus
and I'm God he says
ripping the cord out of the speaker
as I take another drink of wine
absolutely screwed.

I Am the Boustrophedon—

iPhone in one hand

rehto eht ni doohnam

Janus Narcissus Ouroboros

eman ym eb

love possible

dniwlrig nehw

entwines me

hguone gnol

to generate pain

leef t'nod I

white rain/clear tears

lufsseccus os raseaC

he turns on himself

Community Organization

Never understanding
how fucking one
was fucking all
past lovers I became
married and went
to a movie—

If only they hadn't hurt each other
she weeps on the stairs
back to the cars
revealing

loving one
is loving others
who have broken
her to me.

Shoes Without Laces

After her attempt
she wouldn't wear laces
though surrounded by
infinite other ways
to do it
became her style
of refusing to be
complicit
with the world
ready for the rapture
of the EMT.

Cast of Thousands

You watch your child emerge
from your wife's body then
you take them home and wait
for the idiots to arrive
teachers parents coaches
kids bequeathing borrowed pain
then one night rising
to your retching child you read
in her toy mirror words you forgot
you tattooed on your face:
To know life and its attendant horror
I seek contact with your race.

Pollution

On weekends I load lyric
and racquet onto motorcycle
ride two hundred vertical
yards against dead balls
and envelopes
flowing by in little rivers
and mail submissions/compete
in tournaments at Mulholland Tennis Club.
In three years I haven't won a match
or published a poem
but I have a secret:
I can't afford to remain
a phenomenon
on this slanted plane
soon my body and its
radiant ontologies
will be one.

The Poet Ascends

Having walked the earth and found it
unwalkable I leave you now to prepare
my doorway squat in paradise
which if you've read the Bible closely
has class divisions eviler than earth's
because they're based on prior morality
whose point apparently was always really
a bigger house. Oh yes it will be hell
in heaven but family and other enemies
will be there so at least you have an awkward
fog of harpies to avoid which passes
endless time and even eventually
gives you a kind of sense of purpose.
We are who we are because of what we're not
which for me here is living. I was raised wrong
a hilarious thing to say hovering
above the ground looking down women's
blouses. Dad taught me that talent and perseverance
are what matters Mom that Christlike suffering
is what counts. Did you hear *Be professional* or
Kiss fool ass? I didn't think so! Yes my parents
are idiots that's what I love about them it has me
here regretting what I said about blouses
yet crazy enough to fly away from all of you.
Don't tell my children anything. Only this part
of me is leaving. Another part even now does
the hokey pokey making believe he's a robot
playing make believe because even caregivers
need an imaginative entry into games they're not
really supposed to be playing. I know how that sounds
and don't give a fuck having met other parents.
That's what it's all about:
after being trained to impress only God

and future evaluators of ability who like God
may or may not exist when I saw that
my superiors were stupid I was still
in the South with no options of perspective.
Of course I stopped performing
for everyone which is what the earth calls crazy
when the crazy man in question isn't dribbling
on his shirt which I would gladly do if I thought
it would annoy someone I dislike.
Yes I'm leaving you dopes worried
about getting into preschool and whether you
can keep your house. I intend to be homeless
in heaven sleeping in the doorways of mansions
inhabited by the previously morally superior—
no need to be good now! Ensconced baby! What's that?
Am I worried about leaving the atmosphere? Oh no dumbass
and thank you for your support. This asshole logic
I'm only too delighted to escape.
Clearly I'm flying off on faith.
The only ones among you with faith
are the desperately sad because you live
in constant shock at how horrible life here is.
Happy people are groovy with horror
having adjusted their hearts to keep time.
So if I must explain the obvious to dumbfucks
when I reach space I will collapse
into a single unfeeling atom
traveling at medium speed to Wonderland. Capiche?
Once there I will slightly less sadly expand
into the tennised torso you see above you now
knowing he's gone on too long. I hadn't expected
to give a toast but my wife's wailing
sirenized the fire department so I wafted
to witness I'm not beating or raping but
zooming to freedom and transient eternity.
Fuck you all motherfuckers.

[ENTANGLED IN POWER LINES AND ELECTROCUTED.]

Left Eye

Since the sundown has nothing on you

wear only my hands.

Momento mori

Life's too short to appreciate, it does no good to remember you will die. Your thoughtless bones say when inside. Raised by morbid Southern uncles to keep mortality in mind, I entered an Ivy League mental institution enclosed in razor wire. Having spent youth imagining regretting having lost it, on the verge of its disappearance I tried to feel it by touching every passing female and failed by succeeding. En and outraged, one shattered glass and phones, conjuring sirs of the surveillance class, who counted pipes, sniffed bottles, pressing me to press a charge. I pressed pills into my mouth. When some passing females reached back for my unfelt life in the institution, goggle eyed orderlies said I was crazy to be crazy. What made me crazy was not taking everything for granted, wisdom of Eden, ignorance forgot.

Pesticide

Dawn swimming deserves
a film of poison
peach fuzz on a kidney
made of glass.
Naked as motivation
viscera willfully neglected
party guests gone
down County Road 89
young woman leaving
satin robe
slipping as archaeologist
into wreckage of my love
cramming me with skeletons
of future ultrasounds
her backward fingers
spelling *if God is dead*
so is the pilot
holding the hatch open
with his frozen mind.

Balls

Of course they're the origins
so obvious so ugly
so easily hurt.
They suggest symmetry
they author the body's symmetry
yet they are not symmetrical.
Could anyone argue
that every ordered ideal
was not born in them?
When a woman takes them
tenderly in hand
she describes each churning second
of our soft and wrinkled kind:

generosity is required.

Deepwater Horizon

If we were cynical
and had given up the game
we would obscure our poems
with what passes now
for poetry.
We know the rage of futility
we have writhed in various nets.
Hope relies on hopelessness.
We are never hopeless.

Florid Vim

Headed into ninth
Terry Morgan and I
stood at crossroads:
Spanish or French.
As soon as I heard
Janet Porter say Spanish
is more practical
French it was.
Because I met Terry
in that language
I can say his instinct
for absurdity was
identical to mine.

Madame King was barely forty
barely illegal
not accredited.
In 1980s rural Arkansas
having visited New Orleans
was enough.
She had us roll our Rs
into trash cans
you can't improve Arkansas
for accidental symbolism
or finding your orphan brother
seated next to you
because of your last names.
We passed scraps to each other
that read *This* and *That*
asking as seriously as possible
Have you seen *This*?
I am most certain you have yet
to concede an incipient consideration

of *That*
as if denied
proper French instruction
we became Victorian gentleman
laughing off empire's
disappearing fleck.
I've still never met anyone
so entitled to selfpity
yet less interested in it
tautly muscled
smart and funny
Terry is the only man I've ever known.

Because we made each other laugh
constantly we formed a band
called Florid Vim
we thought it sounded like a Cure
song and I had a thesaurus in my hands.
For rehearsals to escape
the orphanage exits
guarded by one eyed
Low Church Protestant Evangelicals
he leapt razor wire
by trash cans
into my waiting Chevy Luv
onto Malvern Avenue
into someone else's parents' home.
He risked more in those evenings
than I had yet
now I think it's evened out:
he knew his mother
she didn't want him
she wanted him
but couldn't keep him
she kept him
but couldn't know him
he was alone.

Things got worse
I left
Terry but he found me
after graduation by phone
he was a Chippendale's dancer

Madame King was arrested
for stealing tour guide tips
in France

thief
dancer
singer
son
life is someone else's story

but that laughter
is mine.

Broken Animal

For creation

the gods cannot be forgiven

and no creature

still in the trap

finds peace there.

against trees

one thing you learn
is to suspect
sentimental objects—
countries deer dead siblings
God stately oaks
the world—
beauty itself
an apology

for having nothing else to say
in the eye of the beholder
a liar's confession—
the stark scrub elm
beholding the world through
my brother's broken eye
may find it beautiful
but that doesn't make anything
worth saving

They Know Not What They Do

The *they* offended
being one of them
pretending to fathom
objectivity.

Now that Jesus is
beneath me
I soften
on his arrogance
as if I were a slightly
higher god
tortured
by another power
rising constantly
above.

White Trash

As a boy I planned to be a garbage man
for I thought he worked one day a week.

When I noised my dream
my loved ones laughed
at my lack of imagination

more vast than they could ever know.
If they weren't idiots
they might have heard
what I was singing
my only song ever since:

money is moving
someone else's refuse
slightly around.
Touch it as seldom as you can.

Excremental Poem

Southern crap is magic—
urination and defecation
attend a kind of coronation.
So tender is the sudden Southern
regent fully enthroned
it's impossible not to imagine
whizzy regicide
stool bloodied
by longhaired men
driven to madness
by transgender music
of flushing.
Shameful laws are needed
so that laws of shame
be not superseded.
The body is a scandal
in the South
enchanted land of waste
once where I was born.

barotrauma

perforating
from heaven
godnailed
in middle ear

What are you looking for Daddy?

lightlessness
obscured by garbage
where my howling
downward
sends you higher
into joy

Forgiveness

Being neither god nor government
offspring's authority
not of right and wrong
but of left and right
having listened closely
to preachers' warnings
about judging others
having been forgiven
by those I have not wronged
having been wronged
by the same forgivers
as they declared through triumphant tears
my forgiveness is not required
for they have forgiven themselves
(for the wrong wrongs)
actually believing
everyone is equal
I am no forgiver
more of a prayer
for a heaven
where forgiveness is escaped.

I Am the Muddler—

hard to find

with knives

in backs

of drawers

where you have to feel

for what is there.

Located

I am used

to sacrifice

sweetness

so that it renders poison

palatable.

Sometimes I seem enormous

and shining

guests are impressed.

Sometimes I am ventured

for tasks beyond my power.

When I fail

no one is surprised

for I am the muddler

and was not meant

to dominate the world.

The Death of Loved Ones

Why does the death of loved ones
shatter us more completely
when we're young?
No one's ever thought
he'll live forever
that he's perfect or he knows it all—
death shame and stupidity
are merely worn in different styles
the most popular of which
is Wise Adult.
Misunderstood youth doesn't bother me
as much as does the narcissism
we lose
a little more of every day.
How dare a loved one die
when we're almost rich and famous?
If we absorb this outrage
into our heroic narrative
something of the dead
loved one lives on
a while in our insanity.
It's insane to live
according to a fantasy
of living.
We're all insane especially you
fantasizing this is not a poem fantasizing
it is
fantasizing me
who today cut his hair with Christmas lights.

I wish the dead could read
the dead are my demographic
the dead are not concerned

with prosody or truth.
Perhaps we turn
so humble perhaps we require
faith and reasonable careers
because our childhood fantasies
reveal themselves
to be not only foolish
and common but also fatal.
Then we pour poison grain
into chopped hourglasses
to dream control
over death of dreams
speeding a fatality on
we didn't know existed
but not so quickly we'd recall
the specific tear shape
that finally did us in.

What is grief but worship
what is worship but debasement
love but tyranny
in tandem?

Dictators adored at first
become despised deposed
and hungered for again.
It's not that we learn too much
to be as arrogant as we used to be.
It's that we gather the wrong knowledge
for strengthening the fantasy
that leads on to success.
We weaken into responsibility
into paying debts.
We're polite to fools.
We waste our lives with fools.
We're ashamed

of the dishonest nature of our shame
of how we wait
in lines chuckling with strangers
as if our fuzzy genitalia won't rot
like a mouse
between the oven and the wall
a dead and secret mouse
whose more careless friend
eats the cheese
we tentatively explored.

Eat my dick like a rat does cheese
I believe Too Short says somewhere.
Or is that Eazy E?
Though no longer in the charts
Too Short sill lives
large.
I saw him
on the only channel I receive
exiting a bar
laughing and slapping
a delighted woman's ass
which promptly vanished
into shadows
of a luxury SUV.
Too Short might be broke
what he has with that woman
in shadows might be very sad
but there was a time
when that would not have occurred
to me.
I wasn't less wise then—
I knew I was born to die.
All I've learned
is how to more effectively
disappear it's like

I joined a cult of humility
memorizing arbitrary tales
in a reasonable mythology
of a meaningless survival.
The Tea Party appeals to me
for reasons they do not intend.
How one can dismiss
only parts
of everything
lies beyond my powers of apprehension.
Jesus freakery is more compelling
than the Scientific Method
and almost certainly more sound.
Those raised to hate
also love their raisers.

When I seem wryly pessimistic
I'm looking for a nonlockupable way
to deny reality which is
a 57 Chevy made me.
Those raised in hell
also are pressured to be happy.
No one believes
you don't exist
if you tell them so
over awful wine.
Death is the tyrant
fucked lovers underthrow.
If we were a race of tyrants
if we weren't contentedly tyrannized
death would look as kissable
as liberal democracy.
Perhaps not—
there's no retirement
from softly compounding shame
which is our life's work.

It inspires all our little
daily suicides.
Compounding shame
compounding death—
we want it slow
but we want it.
So when a loved one dies
and we're not young
it doesn't seem so bad.
Maybe we're relieved
there is one dream
likely to come true.

Sports

boy removes television

replaces it with dad

sets dad on fire

whispering *I love you*

Summer Transfer Information Banquet

chemical transfers stain
countertop to drawer
lie transfers truth
authenticity to art
wine transfers ecstasy
anxiety to death
sex transfers face
man to child

no journey possible
without destination
no joy possible
without obscurity
no joining
possible
we hope you will apply

Every piano should have a dead key

a forced rest
in the song
a dead part
where things go wrong
a little cancer
that will spread
until silence is music
and everything is dead.

Forgetting lyrics onstage is like

forgetting your speech to the Pope
which you practiced with your wife
all the way
from Australia to Philadelphia.
The Pope stands before you
like a microphone
shaped exactly like a microphone
his white cap waiting
for your whispered feelings.
Marky Mark also is waiting
listening nearby
symbolizing the world
satirizing its events.
You begin falter wince.
You look at your wife
as if she were a stranger
you don't even want to fuck.
If the Holy Microphone asked you now
what fucking was
you'd have no idea.
You have forgotten everything
the lie inside
every word is gone
dissolving with it
all your loves and dreams.
You have passed into
the sweet silent guiltlessness of death.
If you stay they will remove you
to unpleasant places reserved
for the free and dead.
So you speak sing remember
re entering the world
begging for your bread.

Wolfgang Anthem

going out with mother
        going out with light

going out with enemies
        who are going out with light

going out to dinner
        feasting on a dying light

going out with Mother
        going out with light

Magnetic Fields

Eastsidedrunk
wife out of town
dentist imminent
I encountered Stephin Merritt
at a newsstand in Los Feliz.

He didn't recognize me
from those centuries
in New York when I was one
of a dozen walking with him
across whichever drink he chose.

It was like Jesus
had faked the Ascension
gotten fat
and wandered out to buy a magazine.
I was bald Paul
ten years on.

"What are you doing here?" I said.
"Who are you?" he said.
"I've told so many about you."
Immortal pause pop
messiah gazing down at shoes.

Thus are disciples doomed
to blossom
into embarrassed skeletons
the talent and the gift
no one needs a model for.

John Pugh XI

Cheapest chugged
vodka possible
reasonable for you
lifting my mother's largest
knife to your throat
to drain a goiter.
What was my excuse? I had to watch it?
I didn't really chug
never could despite
reputations earned
less than claimed like a pond
receives flowers no
I pollinated White Russians
appropriate when half
way through *A Space Odyssey*
my bitter tongue carving
caves craving sweet.
Last night Caitlin Thomas
wife of Dylan described
their drinking had me thinking
we were science fiction
honeymooners that weekend in Hot Springs
smoking dope playing ping pong
and songs we had written
on guitars' broken strings
the world and all its surfaces
too small for half our dreams.

Listening to California

for Jason White

Don't get out
of my head much—
babies books TV
at night glass in hand
murdering the dream—
sometimes in darkness
I think of friends
it was impossible to keep
we were too starving
alongside each other's
ruthless bodies
scavenging sent us
to eyelined carcasses
in adjacent fields.

Some nights rolling over
I hear a coyote cry
in hunger and I pause
from the private feast
of my secret life.
I peer into the canyon.

Perhaps it's a friend
come from another field
to sing out to me
I love you.

Then I feel the emptiness
from such assumptions
in the past
and I resume my feasting
free to be as faceless
as any passing scream.

Suicide by Life

I have decided to die
via life—
my children shall be fathered
as every howling atom
of my brother's shattered
corpse drifts
                    away

a

                    l

                                        o

                                                        n

                                                                e.

Happiness is murder.

family life

tonight the stars have come inside

to satirize sadness

throwing naked shadows

on the little rooms

where we hang our skin

tonight our lawsuits dance

without us

to the rhythm of our children's

lengthening bones

and we are immortal

listening to records

Charlie Sheen

"Back at the Plaza, a delusional and high
Charlie went off his rocker and started
spewing the n-word . . . "

Reaching the top
the bottom appeared
more clearly than before—
so clearly it obsessed him.
He became naked
powdered his face
screamed *Inward!*
in the privacy of his public room.
Later when the cops came
he shone so whitely
they covered him with blankets
gathering him further
into the privilege
one pays dearly to escape.

Pike County

I need to start noticing things.
One star shines at dusk
above our hot tub in the hills
I can show that to my daughter
in hopes it will encourage the poetic
all children inherit and most
eventually decline.
I have disappeared
and thus notice little.
I'm like a country singer
songwriter suddenly rich
with nothing to write about
and decades not to do it.
Funny thing is I am
a failed country singer
songwriter well I didn't fail
the singing and writing as much
as the cocksucking.
Who can love a spitter?
He doesn't want the pain inside.
Hunger is the only genre.
George and Dolly
learn starving singers' songs
while stretching in gyms to seem
hungry for fat patrons.
George's trainer is now
Guillermo Worm
who escaped dissection
in my wife's Biology
by switching himself
with a gummy.
Corn Syrup is the name
Corpsey George has given him

pronouncing it *Kuhn Srp.*
Guillermo has been around the block
Guillermo is no spring chicken
Guillermo wears a tracksuit
when he eats away your eyes.
There was a worm on my brother's rainy grave
the other day in Glenwood
where everyone believes everything
on *TMZ* with reason.
I believe everything
I am done doubting
the blackness
of my father's lungs
the loving racist things it's done
to his lost and racing heart
failing in Little Rock
succeeding there too
while I see now more stars
appear above my sleeping daughter.

Once you go black

you never go
back.
The light at the end of the tunnel
is behind you.
You face
revolution
spiral stairs
of earth
leading downward
until they are
comprised
of love
built to fall away.

dark money

pulsing in the pocket

of my brother's favorite suit

broken fee

murmur allow

ants

six feet to grieve—

permanent shiva

cold

homeless

rending wiser

than moaning

Giving

Seated next to the billionaire's wife
at the charity of white feelings
everyone else standing
I struggled under the formless weight
of our conversation.
She asked what I thought about
virtual reality and its
educational implications
obviously invested.
Gifted connectors care not
for their own opinions
but I can't speak to real people
about virtual reality
it's like a cat discussing
catlike reflexes
or when someone calls a banker
a rock star—
anyone paying attention
already wears those masks
and finds the actual masks redundant
so I pretended to be able only
to recall the Brahmin class
not the Untouchables (she was Indian)
and she turned her back to me
for the rest of that touching evening.
Later I walked onto the beach
and didn't touch the moon
wandering fool doing fine.

Listening to Loretta

One must be alive
in order to commit suicide.
The dead do not plan
and so forth.
I have lived my life
in undermines
next to nothing
mind full of cancer.
My third eye shines in darkness.
It is all you see of me
as I go
ever further
away.

Social Media

Let them speak to each other
they are speaking—
moralizing
robots of the prehistoric cults
ancient internet as
garden
I love you
a simple poison
still unborn.
Because it plans to kill me
I will block the world.

Anchor Baby

Two ghosts in purgatory
made an anchor baby.
Because they'd been to grad school
the ghosts loved liminality
and had made a religion of it
which is to say they were afraid
equally of heaven and of hell.
There was something about grad school
those ghosts it attracted
made this religion logical—
fear of failure fear of success
fear of No fear of Yes
fear of Life fear of Death.
What fool wouldn't want to stay
between forever what fool
thinks he takes a side
he can see?

Hence the baby.

No one could say if making life
in such a world was good or evil.
This was the kind of ambiguity
kept the couple getting out of bed
in the afternoon which half
explains the baby's doorway
conception fucking ghosts just un
naked *Weekend at Bernie's* motorboat
audible beyond ancient midterms
slightly read partly stained
wholly graded.

The birth like death
was touch
and go.
Dad worried Mom
wouldn't be
liminal for long.
She survived delivery
to face a shock:

The baby was not a ghost
the baby was real.
Could a living thing remain in purgatory?
It was a contradiction of terms.
As purgatorians texted
the baby unfastened its frenulum
and mixed its mortality with
eternity. This amused
or terrified purgatorians according to depth
of phantom brainhole.
No ghost's superstition mattered
the baby was fine the baby was
reasonable. Some aspects of purgatory it enjoyed—
stark expanses arbitrary fires—
some it didn't (kisses made you colorblind).
The parents were grateful
to the baby for letting them stay
lost ever more thoroughly confused.

After some decades
the baby disappeared
and the parents passed into hell
which after a while they had to admit
through gnashing gums
was preferable to wondering
what might have been
if they were real.

Learning a Language

Everything is beautifully objectified
simplified to the point of absurdity
whose only requirement
is the absence of irony.
In this way irony is arrogance
arbitrary abuse
of privilege randomly acquired
and absurdity is reasonable
tender a gentle hand
to help you on your way.

Praying Again

(to Jesus)
and his precious holy name—
what can whispers do
for my children's little hands?
What might a derivative god
stretching walls
of repressed southern hearts
of the 1980s
mean to my babies' bodies
in the next room
now?
Protect them
please God
you're all I know.

The old are so arrogant

rarely failing
to remind
how fast
it all goes.
How stupid
do they think
we are?

Rapture

Their foreign travels ended

the family took to riding trains

up and down and desertbound

and back in time for dinner.

Even though he disbelieved

in meaning this habit had Dad

sad which was helpful

later when everyone was

gone and sadness never came

as a surprise.

HELP US BURY MY DEAD BROTHER

—sign carried by man in Lafayette, Louisiana

though he doesn't mean a thing
to you every day he means
else to me we can do it we can
bury my dead brother the me
that's dead with shameless eye
him at the kitchen table she
waves to scare away the flies
it takes a village to stuff a village
we've got children now
who only know our corpses
lift us higher overground

—for Marc T. Wise

Milo

Mounting the museum toilet
she asks when she'll be a boy.
I ask when I'll be a girl.
When you go inside Milo
when you come out you'll be a girl.
She swings her legs and looks above me.
Daddygirl. Mommyboy. Brothergirl. Sisterboy.
So the beast in the family
brindle boxer ancient
as her parents' marriage
is finally recognized
as a portal between sexes
modes of being physical states
of love
and I am blind
drying hands in the abyss
grasping for her mind
to guide me.

Is Daddy dancing?

what my daughter says

as I turn away

to wash the dishes

as if everything is

part of the party

and all movement

made by a beloved

love.

Thank you

for your patience as we lived
with your poems.
They bothered us
on the way back
to our bed
despite our affection
for much of what they said
we closed the door
on their daring and finesse
vowing one day to visit
every state of their undress
noting fondly
the dirty way
they smoked our dope
we learned a lot we hope
they make it home.
They can't stay here
but in thirty years
having learned to deride fame
no one will know
them on the road
or dream
how close they came.

Cocktail Hour

Busy with dreams
I had forgotten it existed.
Now the sky—
no the window—
goldens my shoulder
sore from yesterday's
meager exertion.
I am willing to afford ingredients
that were foolish
willing to drink tears
to stay awake and watch
the miracle assemble.
This is not the central sacrifice
no flesh is here consumed.
This is cocktail hour
the click in the track
before the roller coaster
falls.

JASON MORPHEW started life in a mobile home in Pike County, Arkansas. He holds a PhD in English Renaissance Literature from UCLA. As a singer-songwriter he's released albums on the labels Brassland, Ba Da Bing!, Max!, and Unread. He lives in Laurel Canyon and teaches English at UCLA.

Acknowledgments

"Able to imagine nothing" was previously published in *Juxtaprose Literary Magazine*.

"Acute and Chronic" was previously published in *Blood Tree Literature*.

"At the Disneyland Hotel," "After I Write My Dissertation," "Physical Comedy," "*Torment*," "Deepwater Horizon," "The Death of Loved Ones," "Charlie Sheen," "Listening to Loretta," and "Learning a Language" were previously published by *Floating Wolf Quarterly* in my chapbook entitled *In Order to Commit Suicide*.

"Avalanche" is forthcoming in the anthology *Undeniable: Writers Respond to Climate Change* on Alternating Current Press.

"Baby in a Blender" was previously published in *Venus Magazine*.

"Balls" was previously published in *Gigantic Magazine* (NYU) and nominated for a Pushcart Prize.

"*Does James Brown have a penis?*, "Forgiveness," and "Anchor Baby" were previously published in *Soul-Lit*.

"Evangelical Christianity" was previously published in *The Cortland Review*.

"field song" was a finalist for the 2017 Marica and Jan Vilcek Prize for Poetry and was previously published in *Bellevue Literary Review*.

"Forgetting lyrics onstage is like" was previously published as liner notes for my album *Nobody Knows: Live on WNYU, Aug. 1, 1997* (Unread Records and Tapes).

"Giving" is forthcoming in *Carbon Culture Review*.

"Halogen" was previously published in *Third Wednesday Magazine*.

"House of David" was previously published as liner notes for my album *Easy Come: Songs of 2004* (Unread Records and Tapes).

"How I Came to Stay in The Hague of My Heart" and "John Pugh XI" are forthcoming in *Big Muddy*.

"How to Write a Poet's Bio" and "against trees" were previously published by *Public Pool*. "against trees" was also published as liner notes for my album *Vol. 3: Easy Go* (Unread Records and Tapes).

"How to Write a Poet's Bio" was previously published in *Crosswinds Poetry Journal, Vol. II, 2017*.

"Innocence/Perversity," "dead boy," "marriage," "Evangelical Christianity," "Acute and Chronic," *"Does James Brown have a penis?"*, "field song," "reading in darkness," "Anchor Baby," "Halogen," "Forgiveness," "Baby in a Blender," "Cast of Thousands," *"Let's take it apart,"* "Summer Transfer Information Banquet," "family life," "Pike County," "Praying Again," "Milo," "barotrauma," "The Poet Ascends," and *"Is Daddy Dancing?"* were previously published by Poets Wear Prada in my chapbook entitled *What to deflect when you're deflecting.*

"Leslie," "Since the sundown has nothing on you," "family life," and "marriage" were previously published in *Anamesa: An Interdisciplinary Journal* (New York University).

"Listening to California" was previously published in *Santa Fe Literary Review.*

"My Youth" was previously published in *Storm Cellar Quarterly.*

"Never Settle" was previously published in *Foothill: A Journal of Poetry* (Claremont Colleges).

"Passion" and "Cocktail Hour" were previously published in *Blue Fifth Review.*

"Plastic Texas" is forthcoming in *Poor Yorick Journal.*

"Shoes Without Laces" was previously published in *Claudius Speaks.*

"Sports" was previously published by Always Crashing Magazine.

"Thank you" is forthcoming in *Columbia Poetry Review.*

"They Know Not What They Do," "Excremental Poem," and "Pike County" were previously published in *The New Engagement.*

"White Trash" was previously published in *One Person's Trash.*

"Winery" was a finalist in *Naugatuck River Review*'s 8th Annual Narrative Poetry Contest and was previously published in that magazine.

Thank you: Joe Wenderoth, Miller Williams, David Kramer, Carla Mouton, Lonnie Luebben, Helen Deutsch, Lowell Gallagher, and Danny Passman.